Waiting in Joyful Hope

*Daily Reflections for
Advent and Christmas
2011–2012*

Jay Cormier

D1561713

LITURGICAL PRESS
Collegeville, Minnesota

www.litpress.org

Nihil Obstat: Rev. Robert C. Harren, *Censor deputatus.*

Imprimatur: ✠ Most Reverend John F. Kinney, J.C.D., D.D., Bishop of St. Cloud, Minnesota, April 12, 2011.

Cover design by Ann Blattner. Photo courtesy of Photos.com.

In addition to the optional memorial of St. Thomas Becket, there are other optional memorials not noted.

ISSN 1550-803X

ISBN: 978-0-8146-3361-8

Introduction

Seven hundred years before the birth of Jesus, Israel was a defeated shell of a once-glorious nation, a people enslaved and exiled by their Assyrian occupiers. It is to this broken nation that the Advent prophet Isaiah proclaims reason to hope:

Thus says the LORD, your redeemer, the Holy One
of Israel: . . .
Remember not the events of the past,
the things of long ago consider not;
See, I am doing something new!
Now it springs forth, do you not perceive it? . . .
For I put water in the desert
and rivers in the wasteland
for my chosen people to drink,
The people whom I formed for myself,
that they might announce my praise.
(Isaiah 43:14, 18-19, 20-21)

Our God, Isaiah preaches, is a God of beginnings. The God who called our father Abraham to establish our people as God's own, who led our ancestors out of Egyptian slavery, who raised up David to establish our nation is not satisfied by vengeful endings or destruction. God, prophesies Isaiah, seeks reconciliation among all peoples and nations, in every time and place. God invites us to begin again, to start over, to re-create, to do *something new*.

"Perceiving" the new thing God is constantly doing is the challenge of Advent. In the Lectionary readings for Advent and Christmas, we "perceive"—"behold," as Gabriel and heaven's angels call Mary and Joseph and the shepherds to do in the gospel narratives—God beginning a new genesis; gathering the people for a new exodus out of enslaving fear and into liberating hope; establishing a new kingdom of justice and peace in which the poor will have their "fill" while the rich are sent away "empty," the powerful and arrogant will be toppled, and humility and servanthood will be exalted.

The reflections in this year's edition of *Waiting in Joyful Hope* are images and stories of this "new something" God continues to do in our own lives. May these pages help you this Christmas to realize in your own hearts and homes the eternal "newness" of God's reconciling love.

FIRST WEEK OF ADVENT

Short Nights

Readings: Isa 63:16b-17, 19b, 64:2-7; 1 Cor 1:3-9;
Mark 13:33-37

Scripture:
"Be watchful! Be alert! . . .
 you do not know when the lord of the house is coming,
 whether in the evening, or at midnight,
 or at cockcrow, or in the morning." (Mark 13:33, 35)

Reflection: Most of us shudder remembering the "all-nighters" we pulled in college—cramming all night for that eight-thirty exam, finishing that paper due to a professor by ten o'clock in the morning. Before we realized it, the fourteen weeks of the semester were over—and a mountain of papers had to be completed and exams passed. So, compelled by the fear of flunking out and fortified by caffeine, we read and memorized and typed and highlighted until dawn.

Did you ever find yourself driving all night for an important meeting? Last minute complications or a canceled flight meant driving until dawn to be there on time.

Or you've had to be up early for an appointment or meeting. You're so afraid of oversleeping or so keyed up over your presentation or the meeting's outcome that you wake up every twenty or thirty minutes. You eventually accept the reality that you will not be getting much sleep this night until the meeting is over and done.

And many of us know the anxiety of keeping vigil all night at the bedside of someone we love: the couple awaiting the birth of their child, the spouse pacing anxiously in the hospital waiting room, family members offering what comfort they can as a loved one slips into eternity. After a long night, life is transformed as morning dawns.

These "short nights" we have all kept are all experiences of Advent, the first season of the liturgical year that focuses on the last days. Our lives are a constant Advent: The precious and limited time we live is but a "short night" in which we have much to do and complete before the morning of eternity dawns. Advent calls us to stay awake and not sleep through the opportunities life gives us to discover God and the things of God. Advent calls us to "watch," to pay attention to the signs of God's unmistakable presence in our lives, to live every day of our lives as a gift from God.

Meditation: In what ways have you been most recently reminded how brief and precious life is?

Prayer: Come, Lord, into the Advent of our lives. Come, open our eyes that we may see your hand in all things. Come, fill our hearts with a spirit of humble gratitude that we may realize the gift of our days. Come, illuminate the paths we walk with the light of your wisdom as we journey to your dwelling place.

Improbable Faith

Readings: Isa 2:1-5; Matt 8:5-11

Scripture:
The centurion said [to Jesus] in reply,
  "Lord, I am not worthy to have you enter under my roof;
  only say the word and my servant will be healed."
    (Matt 8:8)

Reflection: It is as improbable a meeting as one could imagine: a centurion pleading to a Jewish rabbi on behalf of a servant. But that is exactly what takes place in today's gospel.

The centurion is an officer of the Roman force occupying Palestine. He has been trained to maintain control by fear and intimidation as well as by the sword. He is despised by the Jewish populace.

The servant is more accurately a slave. In the eyes of the world, he is considered property. He possesses nothing—not even an identity—of his own. By the conventions of the time, the servant's plight should be of little concern to the centurion.

But the centurion possesses a much greater view of humanity than those who witness the encounter. His compassion and gratitude for his critically ill servant enables him to put his stature and authority on the line and approach

Jesus for his help. He is able to see in this Jesus the love of God before him. Jesus assures him that his "faith"—a word that the centurion probably would not use himself—will not be disappointed.

The centurion in Matthew's gospel mirrors the new genesis God initiates in Christ. The centurion—among the least likely of witnesses to Christ—possesses a faith that is not confined to creeds and dogmas but beholds all of humanity as the very reflection of God's goodness. The centurion dares to hope in the transforming grace of God—grace that heals, grace that reconciles, grace that opens hearts and minds to create a world centered in God's peace and justice.

May we possess the unlikely faith of the centurion: faith that creates peace not as the absence of conflict but as an attitude of honor and respect for all as sons and daughters of God; faith that inspires the "beat[ing of] swords into plowshares" for the building of God's kingdom of justice (today's reading from Isaiah); faith that refuses to allow conflict to derail or detract us from the holy work of reconciliation and healing.

Meditation: In what ways can your belief in a God who is Father of all transform your attitudes toward others?

Prayer: Lead us, O Lord, on our Advent journey to your holy mountain. Illuminate our perspective with your vision of peace so that master and servant, parent and child, teacher and student, owner and worker may embrace your reign where all are honored as your children and welcomed as brothers and sisters in your Christ.

New Eyes

Readings: Isa 11:1-10; Luke 10:21-24

Scripture:
"Blessed are the eyes that see what you see." (Luke 10:23b)

Reflection: It may have happened in a chemistry lab or a writing class or an economics seminar, or at your first guitar lesson, or when your grandfather taught you how to cast a fly rod.

The moment you first saw a living cell under a microscope, the cosmos became an exciting place of wonder and discovery.

The first time you were able to strum three guitar chords in succession, your life had a soundtrack.

That early morning when you cast a fly on a brook in springtime under the watchful eye of grandpa, you embarked on a lifelong friendship with nature.

After the writing instructor showed you how to structure sentences and paragraphs to create moods, heighten suspense, or make readers laugh, you never wrote or read a story the same way again.

We have all had those moments—some funny, some painful—when our spouses, our children, our friends showed us something about ourselves that we never realized before, and our lives have not been the same since. We have all had the experience of learning something innovative, of coming to a new understanding of some concept or idea, of having our eyes opened to the different, the possible, the transforming, and we have never looked at our world the same way again.

In this season of Advent, Jesus calls us to do exactly that: to see the world around us with the eyes of God. Faith begins with realizing the touch of God in every molecule of creation, the compassion of God in every loving relationship, the justice of God in every ethical and moral decision. Christ and the Advent prophets urge us to pay attention: to pay attention for the voice of God, the hand of God, the love of God in every joy and sorrow, in every pain and trauma, in every victory and setback.

Like the experiences of the future chemist, the novice guitarist, the fledgling writer, may we embrace an Advent sense of attentiveness and watchfulness in order to behold the beauty and wonder and grace of God's presence in every moment of our lives.

Meditation: Where did you see God's presence in an unexpected place or moment?

Prayer: Open our eyes this Advent, O God, to see your love in our midst, and illuminate our hearts to realize your compassion reconciling our broken lives and healing our hurting world. Animate our spirits with your grace, enabling us to see and embrace the opportunities we have to be prophets and heralds of your justice and peace that we have been blessed to see in our midst.

November 30: Feast of Saint Andrew
(Catholic Church)

Wednesday of the First Week of Advent
(Episcopal Church)

"Sir, We Would Like to See Jesus . . ."

Readings: Rom 10:9-18; Matt 4:18-22

Scripture:
As Jesus was walking by the Sea of Galilee, he saw two
    brothers,
    Simon who is called Peter, and his brother Andrew,
    casting a net into the sea; they were fishermen.
He said to them,
    "Come after me, and I will make you fishers of men."
    (Matt 4:18-19)

Reflection: Today, we celebrate the feast of the apostle Andrew, Peter's brother.

As is the case with just about all of Jesus' apostles, we know very little about Andrew. From what we do know, from John's gospel especially, Andrew was part of Jesus' inner circle. He was the entry point for people to meet Jesus. According to John's gospel, Andrew was a disciple of John the Baptist who introduced the young fisherman to Jesus. Andrew immediately ran and told his brother Peter, "We have found the Messiah!" and brought Peter to meet Jesus. In John's account of Jesus' feeding of the crowd, it is Andrew who finds the boy with the five barley loaves and two pieces of fish and brings him to Jesus. And just before Jesus' death, a group of Greek Jews ask Philip, "Sir, we would like to see Jesus." Philip, in turn, took them to Andrew who brings them to meet Jesus.

As the current generation of Jesus' disciples, we are called to be an entry to Jesus for others. As Andrew took others to Jesus, we take on, in baptism, the same work of bringing others to Christ: in our love, others can come to know the love of Jesus; in our compassion and caring, others can find hope and strength in the reconciling peace of Christ the healer; in our struggle to live the Gospel with integrity and faithfulness, others can hear and see the Word of God made flesh.

Meditation: In what realistic, practical ways can you be an entry point for others to meet Jesus?

Prayer: O Lord, help us to become Andrews in our time and place. May we become doors for others to enter the life of your love, entry ways for others to discover your forgiveness and mercy, places where others may find rebirth and hope.

December 1: Thursday of the First Week of Advent

Just in Front of the Butter and Leftover Chicken

Readings: Isa 26:1-6; Matt 7:21, 24-27

Scripture:
"Everyone who listens to these words of mine and acts on them
will be like a wise man who built his house on rock."
(Matt 7:24)

Reflection: Years from now, when archaeologists and sociologists seek to study our culture and the intricacies of life in the first decades of the twenty-first century, perhaps their best source of information will not be found in libraries, museums, or other such depositories of information and data.

To find out what we really are all about, they should study our refrigerator doors.

The refrigerator door is the place where many an over-scheduled family keeps their master calendars of who has to be where and when. It's the place where busy parents and children communicate with one another through Post-it Notes. It's the place where the cartoons that make us laugh are shared, where photographs of important memories are displayed, where words of wisdom that have moved us and touched us are cut out and kept before us.

10   *First Week of Advent*

Thanks to the effect of magnet to metal, our refrigerator doors chronicle our lives, our belief systems, our goals, and our dreams. What we really believe, what is really important to us, is right there in our kitchens for all the world to see, on the way to the mayonnaise.

Advent challenges us to take a look at our "refrigerator doors," day planners, and journals to see what makes us who we are, on what ethical and moral principles we have built and continue to rebuild our lives. These days before Christ's coming call us to center our lives on the "rock" of God's peace and compassion that is our protection against the storms that batter every house and heart.

Meditation: What is the most important item on your refrigerator door (or display board or calendar book) at present and how can it be an experience of bringing Advent hope to your family?

Prayer: O God, may awareness of your goodness and faith in your providence be the rock on which we build our lives. Open our hearts and spirits to hear you in the voices of one another. Help us to confront the pain and hurt our selfishness causes those we love, to understand how our failure to love and forgive batters the houses we have built for our families. By your wisdom and grace, may we realize that in life's most destructive storms you are with us in the love and forgiveness of family and friends.

Do You Still Believe?

Readings: Isa 29:17-24; Matt 9:27-31

Scripture:
When [Jesus] entered the house,
   the blind men approached him and Jesus said to them,
   "Do you believe that I can do this?"
"Yes, Lord," they said to him.
Then he touched their eyes and said,
   "Let it be done for you according to your faith."
      (Matt 9:28-29)

Reflection: As a child gets older, the question this time of year from friends and family members to parents is, "Does Bobby still believe? Does Meaghan still believe?"

   But just as Jesus asks the two blind men who seek to be healed, Jesus asks us "big kids" every Advent:

   Do you believe? Still? Do you believe in the magic of Christmas?

   Do you still believe in the constant and unfailing love of God?

   Do you still believe that peace is possible among all men and women of good will?

   Do you still believe that we can restore our homes and communities by forgiveness and reconciliation?

Do you believe in Isaiah's prophecy that the blind will see, the lame will walk, the poor will rejoice, the tyrant will be banished?

Do you still believe in Gabriel's revelations to Mary and Joseph and Zechariah, in the angels' good news to the shepherds, in John's baptism at the Jordan: that God's love is present in our midst this very day?

Do you still believe in the miracles you can work this Christmas?

The season of Advent speaks to us of a profound mystery that is often lost in the shopping and decorating, the gift-giving and merrymaking. The magic of Christmas is that the mercy and compassion of God becomes human for us in the person of Jesus: Jesus the teacher, the healer, the worker of wonders, the risen One.

So do you believe . . . still?

Meditation: What part of the Gospel do you struggle with most to continue to believe?

Prayer: Christ our Redeemer, heal us of our doubts and fears, our cynicism and despair, so that we may always believe in your loving and saving presence in our midst in every time, in every place. By your light and grace, may we continue to live in the Advent hope of the coming of your reign of justice and mercy.

December 3: Feast of Saint Francis Xavier
(Catholic Church)

Saturday of the First Week of Advent
(Episcopal Church)

The Search for the Magic Mustard Seed

Readings: Isa 30:19-21, 23-26; Matt 9:35–10:1, 5a, 6-8

Scripture:
Jesus sent out these twelve after instructing them thus,
    "Go to the lost sheep of the house of Israel.
As you go, make this proclamation: 'The Kingdom of
    heaven is at hand.'" (Matt 10:6-7)

Reflection: In his landmark book *When Bad Things Happen to Good People*, Rabbi Harold Kushner relates an old Chinese tale about a woman whose only son died. The grief-stricken woman pleaded with a monk renowned for his holiness for some prayer or magical incantation to bring her son back to her. Instead of sending the poor woman away or trying to reason with her, the monk said, "Fetch me a mustard seed from a home that has never known sorrow. We will then use it to drive the sorrow out of your life."

The woman set off at once in search of such a mustard seed. She came first to a splendid mansion. Knocking on the door, she inquired of the family, "I am looking for a home that has never known sorrow. Is this such a place? It is very important to me."

"You've certainly come to the wrong place," they replied and began to relate all the sad events their family had endured. The woman said to herself, "Who is better able to help these poor unfortunate people than I who have had misfortune of my own?" She stayed with the family to provide what comfort she could and then continued on her search.

But wherever she stopped, whether hovel or palace, she heard story after story of misfortune and tragedy. The woman soon forgot about her quest for a "magic" seed as she continued to help the families she met put their lives back together. She never realized that in her search for comfort and consolation for herself, she found it in her own life by the understanding and kindness she brought to others.

All of us experience sorrow, grief, and despair in our lives. As he sent the Twelve to proclaim God's kingdom, Jesus sends forth every disciple of every time and place to go before him to be messengers of God's reign of peace, compassion, reconciliation, and hope. Such is the work of faith, the call of discipleship. As the grieving woman discovers in her search for the magic seed, it is in extending such blessings to others that we are blessed in return.

Meditation: Is there someone you know to whom you can bring a "mustard seed" of consolation and support this Advent?

Prayer: O God, giver of all good things, may we proclaim your coming this Advent in everything we do. May the healing and compassion we struggle to bring to those we love and our work for justice and peace for all people reap the harvest of your kingdom.

SECOND WEEK OF ADVENT

December 4: Second Sunday of Advent

Advent in Cell 92

Readings: Isa 40:1-5, 9-11; 2 Pet 3:8-14; Mark 1:1-8

Scripture:
John the Baptist appeared in the desert
proclaiming a baptism of repentance for the forgiveness
of sins. (Mark 1:4)

Reflection: Dietrich Bonhoeffer, the renowned Lutheran pastor, preacher, and theologian, was one of the most outspoken Christian voices raised in opposition against Adolph Hitler and the Nazis during World War II. His adamant resistance led to his arrest in April 1943 and his execution two years later. He was thirty-nine.

Shortly before his arrest, Bonhoeffer became engaged to Maria von Wedemeyer. During the two years of his incarceration, Dietrich and Maria exchanged hundreds of letters. Facing his first Christmas in prison in 1943, Dietrich wrote to his beloved Maria: "A prison cell like this, in which one watches and hopes and performs this or that ultimately insignificant task, and in which one is wholly dependent on the door's being open from outside, is a far from inappropriate metaphor for Advent."

In another letter, Bonhoeffer wrote of celebrating Christmas in his new circumstances:

I used to be very fond of thinking up and buying presents, but now that we have nothing to give, the gift God gave us in the birth of Christ will seem all the more glorious; the emptier our hands, the better we understand what Luther meant by his dying words, "We're all beggars, it's true." The poorer our quarters, the more clearly we perceive that our hearts should be Christ's home on earth.

From a prison cell, a young pastor proclaims the uncompromising hope and unconditional love of Advent. Christ comes to release us from the fears, doubts, cynicism, and despair that imprison us; his Gospel of compassion and forgiveness are the keys to the cell doors.

These days of Advent also invite us to embrace the poverty of the Christ Child who comes to illuminate the poor stables of our own lives with the light of God's hope and grace. Before God we are all "beggars" who have been given the gift of life, not because of anything we have done to merit it, but only because of the limitless love of God. In embracing Christ's emptiness to become one of us, may we make of our homes and hearts a dwelling place for the God who comes with compassion that heals and peace that liberates.

Meditation: What gift can you give to another person that comes from your "poverty" rather than your wealth?

Prayer: Come, Lord Jesus, and release us from our prisons of fear and disappointment; fill our empty spirits with your compassion and grace. May forgiveness and reconciliation be the gifts we give this Christmas; may justice and charity be the songs we sing to welcome your birth in our midst.

To Be Possible

Readings: Isa 35:1-10; Luke 5:17-26

Scripture:
[Jesus] said to the one who was paralyzed,
"I say to you, rise, pick up your stretcher, and go home."
   (Luke 5:24)

Reflection: The teacher asked her second grade class what each student wanted to be when he or she grew up.

"A football player," "a doctor," "a policeman," "a fireman," "an astronaut," "a teacher," came the answers from all over the classroom.

Every second grader responded, except Timmy. Timmy just sat quietly at his place.

So his teacher said to him, "Timmy, what do you want to be when you grow up?"

"Possible," Timmy replied.

"Possible?" asked the confused teacher.

"Possible," Timmy said.

"Timmy, what do you mean, you want to be 'possible'?"

"Well," Timmy explained, "my mom is always telling me that I'm impossible. So when I get big, I want to be possible."

The Gospel is about being "possible," about realizing in the Advent of our lives the grace of God enabling us to become people of compassion and justice. In every healing he performs, Jesus does more than heal a physical ailment—Jesus restores broken hearts and re-creates lives mired in the "impossibilities" of despair, fear, and sin. Christ enables us to make possible in our own lives all that he taught and lived—that love, compassion, generosity, humility, and self-lessness will ultimately triumph over hatred, bigotry, preju-dice, despair, greed, and death.

Jesus calls all of us to pick up our "mats" and "rise and walk" and be "possible."

Meditation: What hope do you hold that you would do anything to realize? What would be required of you to make that wish "possible"?

Prayer: Christ our Redeemer, reconcile us to God and to one another. Pull us out of our fears and disappointments, our feelings of inadequacy and worthlessness, our self-centeredness and narrow-mindedness, in order to realize the possibilities of re-creating our lives and our world in the peace and wholeness of your presence among us.

December 6: Tuesday of the Second Week of Advent

Christmas Presence

Readings: Isa 40:1-11; Matt 18:12-14

Scripture:
"If a man has a hundred sheep and one of them goes
     astray,
   will he not leave the ninety-nine in the hills
   and go in search of the stray?" (Matt 18:12)

Reflection: 'Tis the season of Christmas presents. You're probably working through your own gift list today.

But what about Christmas *presence*?

It's more than a play on words; it's the very focus of the Christmas mystery. It's hard to imagine: the God who sparked the first molecule of creation, whose very breath gives and sustains the life of every man, woman, and child, becomes present to us by becoming one of us. God embraces humanity in all its messiness, imperfections, failures, and poverty—and by that presence enables us to transform human frailty and failure into holiness and completeness.

So make this Christmas about Christmas *presence*: Make time to be with those you love; celebrate this season as a family, a community, a parish; welcome one another into the Bethlehem of your kindness, to the Nazareth table of your generosity.

Christmas *presence* is not easy. It demands shutting off, unplugging, powering down, and breaking out of our self-

22   *Second Week of Advent*

centered domain and embracing others in humble generosity and joyful welcome. Your *presence*—to talk, to share, to break bread, to comfort—could be the best *present* you give, and receive, this Christmas.

Meditation: How can you make this holiday season a celebration of *presence* as well as *presents*?

Prayer: Christ our Shepherd, in the midst of these busy days, help us to make time to seek out the lost, bring home the prodigal, and make places for the forgotten and ignored. This Christmas, may we rediscover the joy of family and friends and reconnect, with gratitude and joy, with those whose love and support are reflections of your presence in our lives.

December 7: Saint Ambrose
(Catholic Church)

Wednesday of the Second Week of Advent
(Episcopal Church)

The Joy of Giving,
the Lightness of Another's Happiness

Readings: Isa 40:25-31; Matt 11:28-30

Scripture:
"For my yoke is easy, and my burden light." (Matt 11:30)

Reflection: David's dad was a big Green Bay Packers fan. Every Sunday David and his dad would watch the game together, sharing a big bowl of popcorn and Coca-Colas. Dad, who played linebacker in high school, explained to David the intracies of the game.

The Christmas that David was eight years old, he decided to get his dad a new Packers cap for Christmas. David saved some of his birthday money, put aside some of his allowance, did errands and small jobs for neighbors. And Christmas morning, under the tree, Dad found a box with a brand new Green Bay Packers cap. Dad was delighted.

And so was his son.

It was the first Christmas gift David had ever given. Dad's delight when he put on his new Packers cap made David happier than any of the gifts David received that Christmas morning. It was the best twenty dollars David would ever spend.

Jesus invites us to embrace the joyful sense of fulfillment that can only be realized from "learning" from his example of humility and gratitude, to take on his "yoke" of humble, joyful service to one another as we journey together to the dwelling place of God. As David discovers in his first experience of Christmas gift-giving, we proclaim the Gospel most effectively and meaningfully not in words but in the generosity and compassion we extend to others. In our smallest acts of kindness, in our humblest work of justice, we make the Word of God a living reality in our time and place.

Meditation: What gifts will you give this Christmas that will give you, the giver, the most joy?

Prayer: Lord Jesus, may your Spirit of humility and compassion inspire our gift-giving this Christmas and enable us to take on your "yoke" of selflessness and "burden" of reconciliation in every season of the new year.

*December 8: Immaculate Conception
of the Blessed Virgin Mary*
(Catholic Church)

Thursday of the Second Week of Advent
(Episcopal Church)

The Vow of "Yes"

Readings: Gen 3:9-15, 20; Eph 1:3-6, 11-12; Luke 1:26-38

Scripture:
"Behold, I am the handmaid of the Lord.
May it be done to me according to your word." (Luke 1:38)

Reflection: In her best-selling book *Acedia & Me: Marriage, Monks and a Writer's Life*, Kathleen Norris tells the story of her marriage to David and the challenges of commitment in the midst of her husband's debilitating illness and death. She writes:

> My marriage is the one thing I kept saying yes to, even when it hurt to do so. . . . The very nature of marriage means saying yes before you know what it will cost. Though you may say the "I do" of the wedding ritual in all sincerity, it is the testing of that vow over time that makes you married.

To say yes to our vow as a spouse, to our vocation as a parent, to our friendships and commitments is hard, constant work. Today we celebrate just such a yes: Mary's yes to God's call to her to become what the Eastern church calls *Theoto-*

kos—the "bearer of God." Despite her understandable confusion and fear, Mary's yes—a yes of commitment and constancy—is offered in complete faith and trust in the God of all that is good. And because of her yes, the Christ event, the new Genesis, the second creation begins. In baptism, we say yes to God's call to the ministry of reconciliation, yes to becoming prophets of justice, yes to taking on the work of establishing God's reign in our time and place.

It is a yes that we affirm every day of our lives, in our marriages, in our families, in our work, in every encounter and relationship. It is a yes that is often demanding and difficult, exhausting and defeating. In her own yes to God, Mary our sister becomes the model for our own yes to God and our yes to one another.

Meditation: What is the most important and difficult thing you say yes to every day of your life? What makes your yes so difficult? How does Mary's own yes make your response easier?

Prayer: Gracious God, may we have the faith and trust of your daughter Mary to say yes to your call to us to make your presence real in our own time and place. May our hearts say yes to the gift of your Son; may our spirits say yes to your invitation to bring that gift to our Advent world.

December 9: Friday of the Second Week of Advent

Seeking Advent Patience

Readings: Isa 48:17-19; Matt 11:16-19

Scripture:
"[W]isdom is vindicated by her works." (Matt 11:19)

Reflection: We are not a very patient people.

We can't spare the time to stop and catch our breath. Quiet unnerves us; silence is a sure sign that something is wrong; reflection and thoughtfulness are luxuries. We do not live in the moment—we live in the *next* moment.

We need to be constantly connected, online, and plugged in.

We are terrified of being bored.

We are in a constant hurry—and yet we do not get very far.

We struggle to walk between the austere, demanding John at the Jordan and the Jesus who welcomes and forgives all.

Too often we let our fears and doubts, our cynicism and fatalism, affect our decision making. We are defeated by what is *not* rather than inspired by what *could be*.

For all our technology, we are disconnected.

For all our global outreach, we know little beyond our own little plot of earth.

For all our education, we fail to realize what is good and right in our midst.

Advent calls us to patience—not patience that passively accepts without complaint whatever disappoints us, but patience that is certain in the hope of better things to come. In criticizing the fickleness of this "generation," Jesus points out that wisdom begins with such patience: to stop, to reflect, to see what is hidden, to listen with the heart. These days of Advent are a microcosm of our lives, revealing to us the preciousness of time and confronting us with our mortality. May these days teach us to realize the sacred in our lives, to behold God's love in the midst of our family and friends, to embrace the patience of Advent in order to see our lives and world through the eyes of God.

Meditation: What issues and concerns most test your patience? Reconsider how you respond and how you view the situation in question.

Prayer: Lord of Advent, may your wisdom illuminate our eyes and open our hearts to behold your presence in our midst. Help us to embrace the grace of Advent patience, that we may stop and behold your compassion and mercy in our days and transform our lives in the peace and hope of your dawning at Christmas.

"Do-aye"

Readings: Sir 48:1-4, 9-11; Matt 17:9a, 10-13

Scripture:
"Elijah will indeed come and restore all things;
   but I tell you that Elijah has already come." (Matt 17:11-12)

Reflection: In 2007 the Buddhist monks and nuns of Burma (now Myanmar) faced down the powerful generals who had devastated their country with the only "weapon" they possessed: wooden bowls.

In better times, monks and nuns—revered by the Burmese as the country's highest moral authority—walk through the streets carrying wooden begging bowls, collecting alms and donations. To place a gift in a monk's bowl is considered making a gift to God. But during the pro-democracy demonstrations, the monks refused to accept alms from members of the military, a refusal known as "turning over the rice bowl." The gesture amounts to excommunication. The message to the military: *Your brutality and oppression have put you at odds with the ways of God.* In the Myanmar language, the word for "boycott" comes from the words for holding the bowl upside down.

Despite being detained, tear-gassed, and beaten by government troops, the monks continued their nonviolent march for democracy for several months. They were joined by many Burmese, as well. As they walked through the streets, they carried banners reading *Loving kindness*; the monks and people who joined them chanted *Do-aye*, "It is our task."

In their witness to justice and equality in their homeland, the monks and nuns of Myanmar mirrored for their people and the rest of the world the justice and equality of the reign of God. With the same fire for the things of God, Elijah prophesies to Israel; with the same passionate hope that better things are to come, John the Baptizer proclaims God's reign of justice and forgiveness; with the same selfless sense of servanthood, Jesus gives his life on the cross.

Inspired by Christ's spirit of humility and selflessness, called to be prophets in our own time and place, moved by the sacrifice of men and women like the monks and nuns of Myanmar, may we embrace God's spirit of justice, integrity, and humility and proclaim the uncompromising love of God for all men and women; may we lay claim to the moral authority of humble servanthood that resonates long after fads fade and self-interests prove empty, authority that reflects the humble and selfless compassion of the Easter Christ.

Meditation: What do you embrace as your task to bring the justice of God to your corner of the world?

Prayer: By your grace, O God of Advent, may we take on our *do-aye*, "our task," of proclaiming your compassion and justice in our midst. Ignite in us the fire of Elijah, that we may proclaim, in our own commitment to ethics and morality, your reign of justice and reconciliation. Open our lips to speak the good news of John, that in our own compassion and humility we may proclaim your love in our midst.

THIRD WEEK OF ADVENT

Candles in the Window

Readings: Isa 61:1-2a, 10-11; 1 Thess 5:16-24; John 1:6-8, 19-28

Scripture:
[John] came for testimony, to testify to the light,
   so that all might believe through him. (John 1:7)

Reflection: Under orders from the king, the English armies occupying Ireland in the seventeenth century enforced the suppression of the Irish peasants' "Roman" religion. Priests became outlaws, forced to minister on the run and celebrate the sacraments in secret.

When Christmas came, some Irish families would place burning candles in their windows and leave their doors unlocked. The suspicious English demanded to know the purpose and meaning of this custom. The Irish would explain to the soldiers that the candles were lighted and their doors left open so that Mary and Joseph, looking for a place to stay on this Christmas Eve, might find their way to their homes where they would be welcomed. The English considered this just another silly Irish "superstition" and thought no more of it.

But the lighted candles were actually a signal to any priest in hiding that this was a "safe" house where they could come and offer Mass on this sacred night.

We continue to mark this holy season with lights in our windows, as well as on our doorposts and Christmas trees.

But let our lights be more than mere decorations. Let our lights announce the dawning of the Christ—the light of God's own "work" that shatters the darkness of the long night of sin and alienation; the sacred light that illuminates our vision to realize God's dream of a just world of peace and compassion; the holy light that heals us of our blindness to the pain and anguish, the poverty and suffering of others.

Meditation: What decorations in your home are the most meaningful to you? How do they express the true meaning of Christmas?

Prayer: Christ our light, may the candles and lights we use to decorate this Christmas remind us of your love in our midst. Let the brightness of your love and mercy shine brightly in every season before us; may your light be reflected in our hospitality to all who come to our home during this Christmas season.

December 12: Feast of Our Lady of Guadalupe
(Catholic Church)

Monday of the Third Week of Advent
(Episcopal Church)

Mother and Sister of All

Readings: Zech 2:14-17 or Rev 11:19a; 12:1-6a, 10ab; Luke 1:26-38 or Luke 1:39-47

Scripture:
"And how does this happen to me,
   that the mother of my Lord should come to me?
For at the moment the sound of your greeting reached my
      ears,
   the infant in my womb leaped for joy." (Luke 1:43-44)

Reflection: Today's feast of Our Lady of Guadalupe celebrates the apparition of the Virgin Mary in 1521 to Juan Diego, a Mexican peasant.

The most interesting dimension of the story is the vision of Mary that Juan saw. The Mary who appeared on the hillside near the village of Tepeyac was not the white European Madonna the Spanish conquistadors brought with them to America. The Mary whom Juan saw was a woman of dark skin and Indian features. She wore the dress of a Mexican peasant woman. She spoke not in the Spanish of the occupiers but in the dialect of Juan's people. The stars on her blue mantle and the image of the crescent moon on which she stood were all symbols from Indian culture and folklore. According to chronicles of the appearance, she called herself "Mother of the true God through whom one lives" and wanted her presence to manifest God's love for the suffering native people of the Americas. She expressed her wish that a church be built on the hillside where all may realize God's spirit of compassion and justice in their midst.

The image of Our Lady of Guadalupe mirrors a compassionate God who speaks words of love to all peoples, in all languages, within all cultures. Today's feast reminds us that the mystery of God's becoming human in the person of Jesus is a gift to all of humanity: that God comes to be part of the joys and struggles, the complexities and challenges of the human experience. In the incarnation, God enters the human condition, takes on our flesh, lives our life, and, in doing so, raises the dignity of every human being and makes every human life sacred and holy.

God is with us in our poverty and despair; God walks with us when we are most alone; God speaks in love and compassion that we can comprehend and embrace despite our limitations and confusion.

Meditation: In what ordinary and everyday aspects of your life is the reality of God's love present?

Prayer: Come, Lord, and make your dwelling in our midst. As Mary appeared to Juan Diego as a sister to his people, may we recognize you in our midst in the faces of our own brothers and sisters.

December 13: Saint Lucy
(Catholic Church)

Tuesday of the Third Week of Advent
(Episcopal Church)

The Advent We Hope For

Readings: Zeph 3:1-2, 9-13; Matt 21:28-32

Scripture:
[The parable of the two sons:]
"Amen, I say to you,
    tax collectors and prostitutes
    are entering the Kingdom of God before you."
        (Matt 21:31)

Reflection: Today's gospel usually brings a ready smile to the faces of parents who have sparred with their children over getting the simplest of chores done.

But the two boys in Jesus' little parable today illustrate the gap that can exist between what we say and what we do. Too often the values we say we live are not reflected in the decisions we make; we find ourselves unable to take the first step in the change and conversion we pray for; the faith we celebrate on Sunday is nowhere to be found the other six days of the week.

This season of Advent is a case in point. We want a Christmas that is centered on the Child, but with all the shopping and decorating and partying, we never quite make it to Bethlehem. The humble simplicity of Jesus' coming is overwhelmed by the gilt and the glitz. The light of the Savior is dimmed by the glare of the ornaments and tinsel. By the time the angels invite us to behold the miracle of Jesus' birth, we're too tired to trudge to the manger.

Let's resolve today that, in some small way, we are going to keep Christmas as we pray we will, that we will welcome Christ into our lives in a manner that reflects the hope of our hearts, that we will put some time and energy into making this Christmas a time of healing, of peace, of joy for those we love.

Meditation: What one change can you make to some aspect of your Christmas preparations that can make the season more of an experience of the holy?

Prayer: O God, may your wisdom and grace help us to make these Advent days the season we always pray it will be. By your light, may we see where we may bring your peace; by your compassion, may we eagerly take on the work of bringing justice to birth in our midst.

'Blessed tree of light and kindness'

Readings: Isa 45:6c-8, 18, 21c-25; Luke 7:18b-23

Scripture:
"Go and tell John what you have seen and heard:
the blind regain their sight,
the lame walk,
lepers are cleansed,
the deaf hear, the dead are raised,
the poor have the good news proclaimed to them."
    (Luke 7:22)

Reflection: Among the many myths and legends that surround the tradition of the Christmas tree is the German story of St. Boniface, the eighth-century English missionary who brought the Gospel to Germany. According to one version of the legend, on the night of December 24, Boniface came upon a giant oak tree that was considered sacred to the great pagan god Odin. Priests of Odin were about to sacrifice a young boy who had been tied to the sacred tree. The horrified Boniface seized an axe, cut the boy's lashings, and, with one stroke, felled the giant oak. The onlookers were terrified, waiting for the gods to strike Boniface dead. But nothing happened. They realized immediately that their gods were powerless illusions.

This was not a night of death but of life, Boniface said, for this is the night of Christ's birth. Boniface then pointed to a nearby fir tree and blessed it, proclaiming the evergreen the tree of the Christ Child. He then invited everyone to bring this tree into their homes as a symbol of peace. May Christ's tree, Boniface prayed, not be a shelter for deeds of blood but a gathering place of love and kindness.

Today's beautiful readings speak of a world transformed from barrenness to life, from sickness and fear to healing and hope, from hatred and injustice to love and peace. May our Christmas tree this year, like Boniface's evergreen, be our first planting of a new attitude and vision of kindness, compassion, and reconciliation; may our celebration of Christ's birth be the first stone we use to create a highway for the coming of our God.

Meditation: How can you make your own Christmas tree a symbol of Christ's presence in your family's midst?

Prayer: Christ the Messiah, let your Word take root in us and open us up to the possibilities of re-creating our world in your justice and compassion. Compelled by your Spirit of humble servanthood, may we bring sight to the blind, healing to the sick, your good news to the poor, hope to the despairing, and new life to the dead in spirit.

December 15: Thursday of the Third Week of Advent

Messengers in the Spirit of John

Readings: Isa 54:1-10; Luke 7:24-30

Scripture:
"I tell you,
   among those born of women, no one is greater than John;
   yet the least in the Kingdom of God is greater than he."
      (Luke 7:28)

Reflection: She is the first one at the shelter every morning. She opens up, changes and washes the bed linens, sweeps the floor, and cleans the shower area. She silently goes about her tasks with a joyful dedication that disarms visitors and often causes the staff to forget that she is a volunteer. In the dignity and compassion she extends to those who come to the shelter, she is a "messenger" of the love of God.

Saturday mornings are a special time for him. That's when he meets Kevin, his eleven-year-old "Little Brother." He says he gets as much out of his time with Kevin as Kevin does—the satisfaction that comes from being needed, the joy of giving to another; but to Kevin, his "Big Brother" is a "messenger" of hope.

She never imagined herself as an activist or a political anything before. She was happiest simply being "Mom." But that changed when her bright and beautiful seven-year-old was struck and killed by a drunk driver. Her pain and the pain of thousands of parents like her compelled her to speak out against the injustice and irresponsibility of deaths like her child's and to work for more effective laws and stricter penalties for those who drive impaired by drugs or alcohol. In her work for the safety of other children, she is a "messenger" of the justice of God.

There are many "messengers" of God's love, justice, and hope around us who, as did John, proclaim in their humility and compassion the Good News of God's presence in our midst. In unexpected ways, in works we underestimate, in kindnesses we extend with little thought or effort, we nonetheless proclaim the compassion of God. As we await the coming of the Lord at Christmas, let us recommit ourselves to our baptismal call to be "messengers" of the Lord, witnesses of God's love for all of us as sons and daughters.

Meditation: In what small but significant way can you "proclaim" John's word of reconciliation and forgiveness this Advent?

Prayer: O God, our Maker and Redeemer, make us your "messengers" to all your holy people. May our smallest and invisible kindnesses, our humblest acts of forgiveness and reconciliation, point to your presence in our midst and the beginning of your reign of justice and peace.

December 16: Friday of the Third Week of Advent

The Lights Are on in the Parish Hall

Readings: Isa 56:1-3a, 6-8; John 5:33-36

Scripture:
"John was a burning and shining lamp. . . .
The works that the Father gave me to accomplish,
    these works that I perform testify on my behalf
    that the Father has sent me." (John 5:35a, 36)

Reflection: On a given morning in the parish hall, the teenagers in the confirmation class are packing up winter coats they have collected for the homeless.

Later that day, the hall kitchen buzzes with volunteers preparing soup and sandwiches for the parish's regular turn that night at the downtown soup kitchen.

In the afternoon, a group of moms takes over the space and turns it into an after-school center for kids to come to do homework, enjoy a snack, receive tutoring help, and have a safe place to hang out after school instead of going home to an empty house.

After supper, the knitting group will meet to make prayer shawls for the sick and dying in the parish. Their work is a warm, comforting expression that the suffering and hurting of these brothers and sisters are embraced in the prayers of the community.

It seems the lights never go out in this parish hall. The lamp of God's love continues to burn in the work these parishioners do. In baptism, we are entrusted with the work of God. As witnesses of Christ's resurrection, as the eucharistic community Jesus has formed, we become "burning lamps" of the compassion and justice of God in our midst. Our simplest, unremarkable works of charity are extensions of the sacrament we offer at the Lord's table; our unheralded, unseen efforts to bring healing and hope to others are burning lamps revealing the reign of God that has come.

Meditation: Is there some parish ministry that you have hesitated to contribute to that could use your time or support?

Prayer: Father of compassion, may we become this Advent the prayer we offer to you. Let our works of justice and reconciliation illuminate your love in our midst; let our selfless generosity and humble kindness proclaim the dawning of your Son upon us.

December 17: Saturday of the Third Week of Advent

The "Red Thread"

Readings: Gen 49:2, 8-10; Matt 1:1-17

Scripture:
The book of the genealogy of Jesus Christ,
   the son of David, the son of Abraham. (Matt 1:1)

Reflection: A number of East Asian legends and fairy tales
are based on the "red thread" or "red string." The stories are
centered on the belief that when a child is born an invisible
red thread connects that child's soul to all those—past, present, and future—who will play a part in the child's life. With
every birthday, according to the myth, the thread shortens
and tightens, bringing the child closer to those the child is
destined to meet. According to another version of the legend,
the gods tie an invisible red string around the ankles of men
and women who will one day meet, fall in love, and marry.
The thread may stretch or tangle, the Chinese proverb says,
but will never break.

Today's gospel is the red thread that connects Jesus to
those who came before him and who follow him. The evangelist Matthew reminds us that the thread begins with the
unfathomable love of God and continues through the prophets and remnant of Israel; that same thread also ties us to the
Father and Son and to one another.

The historical accuracy of Matthew's list is dubious, but that is not the evangelist's point. For Matthew, this Jesus is the fulfillment of a world that God envisioned from the first moment of creation—a world created in the justice and peace that is the very nature and substance of its Creator. God's vision threads together desert nomads and kings, shepherds and farmers, craftsmen and peasants, saints and sinners. And the thread connects all of us—and our children and grandchildren and their children and grandchildren. Through Jesus, God has tied all of us together: Abraham and Judah and Tamar and David and Hezekiah and Eliakem and Joseph and Mary of the first Advent to all of us of the second Advent who await the reappearance of God's Christ at the fulfillment of time.

Meditation: In what ways do you feel "connected" to those who have come before you and with those who come after you?

Prayer: God of all creation, let us always feel the pull of the thread that ties us to one another and to you. May its tug remind us that we are all connected to you as your sons and daughters and to one another as brothers and sisters. May its enduring resilience enable us to create your reign of justice and compassion in our moment of history.

FOURTH WEEK OF ADVENT

December 18: Fourth Sunday of Advent

The Bird Prince

Readings: 2 Sam 7:1-5, 8b-12, 14a, 16; Rom 16:25-27; Luke 1:26-38

Scripture:
And the angel said to [Mary] in reply,
  "The Holy Spirit will come upon you,
  and the power of the Most High will overshadow you.
Therefore the child to be born
  will be called holy, the Son of God." (Luke 1:35)

Reflection: There is an old Jewish folk tale about a king's son who goes mad: the boy believes he is a bird. He removes all his clothes and goes to live in a tree near the nests of robins and starlings; he refuses to eat normal food or return to his warm, safe room in the castle. His distraught father summons all manner of experts to come and cure the boy, but no physician or sage can help the sad prince.

Then one day a rabbi, a man of great compassion and humility, hears about the plight of the royal family. He comes to the castle and offers his help. The king, desperate for a cure, takes the rabbi to see the prince. The rabbi then does something that no one else had done: he climbs the tree and joins the boy on one of the highest branches and declares that he too is a bird and has come to live in this beautiful tree.

Over time, the rabbi and the prince become friends. The prince begins to trust this old "bird" living in the tree with him; the boy comes to realize that the rabbi is a man of great wisdom and grace.

Gradually the rabbi is able to convince the bird-prince to put on his clothes and return to his home and family.

In today's gospel, God breaks into human history in the birth of Mary's child. God puts aside divinity to climb the tree into which we have escaped in our "madness" and fear. In becoming "birds" like us, in taking on our human condition in all its complexities and challenges, God—in the person of Jesus of Nazareth—shows us how to live fulfilling and grace-filled lives of compassion, forgiveness, and justice.

Meditation: In what ways do you see God affecting the decisions you make?

Prayer: Come, Lord Jesus, Light of God's grace, and illuminate our road to the Father. Come, Lord Jesus, Mirror of God's love, and teach us to reconcile our world in justice and peace. Come, Lord Jesus, Bread of God's life, and feed us with manna of wisdom and righteousness.

December 19: Monday of the Fourth Week of Advent

Speechless

Readings: Judg 13:2-7, 24-25a; Luke 1:5-25

Scripture:
"But now you will be speechless and unable to talk
    until the day these things take place,
    because you did not believe my words,
    which will be fulfilled at their proper time." (Luke 1:20)

Reflection: *We are speechless:* An extraordinary kindness or
an unexpected grace leaves us without words to express our
thanks.

We are speechless: The full impact of what has happened
has not hit us yet. We don't know how to react. We have been
hurt and disappointed one too many times to let our guard
down. We have become too jaded and cynical to trust that
good things can happen. We are too protective of the secure
little world we have created for ourselves and our families
to risk what we don't fully understand or that challenges
our self-centered view of the world.

We are speechless: We are too afraid to speak up or speak
out. There will be repercussions no matter what we say. The
words of our hearts remain stuck in our throats, unable to
be articulated.

Zechariah experiences such speechlessness. Gabriel's news
that he and his beloved Elizabeth would become parents at

their advanced ages is too unreasonable, too impossible, for him to grasp. He has seen too much in his long life; he has learned the painful lessons of the world. His own doubts and fears leave him speechless.

We can understand poor Zechariah's inability to respond. We have been left speechless ourselves. But Advent challenges us to grasp the reality of God's compassion bringing forth life from the seemingly dead, to embrace the idea that our God is a God of limitless and unconditional love that makes even the desert bloom. The dawning of God's Christ illuminates our hearts and spirits with a perspective of the world that begins with a real sense of awe and gratitude at the constantly "new" things God is doing to reconcile us and world to himself.

Meditation: When has some unexpected joy left you without words to express gratitude? In hindsight, what would you have liked to have said?

Prayer: By the light of your grace, O God, may we recognize your presence in every moment of our lives and find the words to express our gratitude and hope. May our Advent journey enable us to trust in your Word dwelling in our midst and take on, with joy, your work of reconciliation and justice.

In God's Own Good Time

Readings: Isa 7:10-14; Luke 1:26-38

Scripture:
Mary said, "Behold, I am the handmaid of the Lord.
May it be done to me according to your word." (Luke 1:38)

Reflection: For months, you have been preparing for a big meeting or major presentation—only to have everything put on hold because a snowstorm shuts down the city.

An afternoon of appointments has to be rescheduled because your child's school called: your seven-year-old has been sent home with the flu.

You and your spouse live your lives on tinder hooks planning and waiting for the birth of your child.

A family's life is turned upside down when his or her MRI reveals a dark shadow.

And in the middle of end-of-the-year reports, final exams, and the biggest sales period of the year comes Christmas.

If you've ever complained that your time is not your own, you're right. It isn't. Time is not ours. It is God's.

The late NBC news anchor and commentator John Chancellor was looking forward to a comfortable retirement when he was stricken with an aggressive form of stomach cancer. Before his death in 1996, he told an interviewer, "Cancer is a reminder of how short a leash you're on. As I read some-where, 'You want to make God laugh? Tell him your plans.'"

Our lives are a series of "interruptions" by God—"annunciations," if you will—in which God focuses our attention on God's love and mercy, compassion and grace, in the midst of our busy lives. God gives us time as a gift and sanctifies that gift by entering time in the person of the Christ. In her faithful acceptance of Gabriel's news, Mary understands that. In the Christmas event, God sanctifies time for eternity; God calls us to live the holiness of time in every season of every year.

May God "interrupt" our Christmas with the true joy of the season, and, like Mary, may we say yes to the interruption; like Mary, may we accept, with gratitude and joy, God's invitation to bring the beloved Son into own our Bethlehems and Nazareths.

Meditation: What "interruptions" or unexpected turns in your life might be seen as "annunciations" of God's presence in your midst?

Prayer: Gracious God, may we possess the faith and trust of your daughter Mary to say yes to your "interruptions" in our lives, when you call us to make your presence real in our own time and place. In our welcoming of your Son into our homes and hearts, may we embrace the Advent meaning of this gift of time you have given us.

December 21: Wednesday of the Fourth Week of Advent

"In Haste"

Readings: Song 2:8-14 or Zeph 3:14-18a; Luke 1:39-45

Scripture:
Mary set out in those days
   and traveled to the hill country in haste
   to a town of Judah,
   where she entered the house of Zechariah
   and greeted Elizabeth. (Luke 1:39-40)

Reflection: Luke writes that after the angel Gabriel departs, Mary travels "in haste" to Zechariah's house.

"In haste." Why the hurry?

Clearly, Mary and her elderly cousin Elizabeth were close. Elizabeth sounds like she must have been a kind of "big sister" to Mary and the other women in the clan. Elizabeth always knew what to do; she would always say the right thing. Mary must have also been concerned for her cousin, who is about to give birth to a child in her advanced age. It's not unreasonable to think that Mary hurries to the hill country in order to see for herself if Elizabeth is really pregnant; that would be Mary's first real confirmation of Gabriel's news.

But it is also clear that Elizabeth was a guide and comfort to her younger cousin. Maybe Mary plans to tell Elizabeth before anyone else in the clan (including Joseph?) her own news. Elizabeth seems to operate on a much different plane than the rest of the family; she has reacted to the news of her own pregnancy with much more enthusiasm and joy than her doubting and terrified husband, Zechariah. Mary knows that Elizabeth will be compassionate in her reaction and wise in her advice to the unmarried and suddenly pregnant teenager. Elizabeth senses the Spirit of God at work in her life and in the life of Mary. In her own joy, Elizabeth transforms her young cousin's anxiety to hope; in her own faith, she helps Mary understand what God is doing. Elizabeth is a woman of remarkable grace and understanding; her ability to see God's mercy in the most desperate of situations and to point to the light of that mercy had to have been a great blessing to Mary and her family. Elizabeth mirrors family at its best.

The meeting between Mary and Elizabeth in Luke's gospel is a beautiful image of the unconditional and unlimited love that binds a family together: love that enables one cousin to put aside her own plight to help the other cousin, compassion that allows the older woman to offer comfort and joy to the younger woman in her anguish. As husbands and wives, as mothers and fathers, as sisters and brothers, God has given us one another to create a safe, welcoming place called family.

Meditation: Who is the Elizabeth in your family? What characteristics of Elizabeth would you like to bring to your own children and siblings?

Prayer: Gracious God, inspire us with the wisdom and grace exhibited by Elizabeth. May the Elizabeths in our own families help us to embrace and be embraced by your grace and your Spirit of love, enabling us to bring your peace and reconciliation to our own hearths and tables.

December 22: Thursday of the Fourth Week of Advent

Turning the World Upside Down

Readings: 1 Sam 1:24-28; Luke 1:46-56

Scripture:
"[T]he Almighty has done great things for me. . . .
He has cast down the mighty from their thrones,
    and has lifted up the lowly.
He has filled the hungry with good things,
    and the rich he has sent away empty." (Luke 1:49, 52-53)

Reflection: A college professor is turning the world upside down. With the help of colleagues she runs a college study program for inmates at a women's prison. Her work is "filling" the souls and imaginations of these women with hope and new possibilities for a meaningful life after prison.

A group of Catholic sisters has formed a project called Solidarity with Southern Sudan. At their hospital, the sisters are establishing a school for health-care workers, with a special focus on midwifery to reduce deaths in childbirth. These women are enabling a country devastated by war and poverty to realize the "promise of mercy" for generations to come.

A high school junior and her family have gone through hard times. Now that her own family is getting back on their feet, she helps other teenagers in the same situation. She connects kids with tutors and counselors; with the help of a local church, she collects donations of everything from used prom dresses to iPods. Perhaps most important of all, she provides a listening ear and a comforting shoulder to kids struggling to keep up. In her extraordinary courage and grace, this young woman is "lifting" up the lowly and filling the hungry and poor with "good things."

These women have taken up the spirit of Mary's *Magnificat*, placing their hope in discovering joy in the God who is filled with mercy and love and not judgment and condemnation, in the promise of good things for the hungry and poor.

Mary's song is the first proclamation of the Gospel of the Christ who comes to reveal the reign of God. She understands and declares what God will do in the child she will bear; she knows that, in the promise she has received from God, history is about to be turned upside down. Mary also realizes that she is herself the first instance of this upside-down future. Mary embodies the good news she proclaims— the Gospel of forgiveness, humble service to others, justice, and, ultimately, resurrection.

Meditation: How can—and should—the spirit of Mary's Gospel canticle turn your world upside down?

Prayer: May Mary's song, O God, become our song of joy and hope this Christmas. Never let us lose hope in your promise of mercy; never let us be imprisoned by despair. May we embrace Mary's faith and sense of hope so that we may transform our world in your compassion and peace, and reimagine our lives in your justice and reconciliation.

December 23: Friday of the Fourth Week of Advent

A Parent's Hope

Readings: Mal 3:1-4, 23-24; Luke 1:57-66

Scripture:
[Zechariah] asked for a tablet and wrote, "John is his name,"
   and all were amazed.
Immediately his mouth was opened, his tongue freed,
   and he spoke blessing God. (Luke 1:63-64)

Reflection: A rabbi was officiating at the naming of a baby for a family who had resettled in the United States from the Soviet Union. The father, a child of the Communist era who was taught to regard religion as illusion and nonsense, looked at his infant daughter and then asked the rabbi, "Rabbi, do you believe in God?"

The rabbi replied that, yes, he did believe in God. He then asked the newborn's father if he believed in God as well.

The father responded, "No, I don't. But I hope *she* will."

The father's hopes despite his doubts mirror those of Zechariah in today's continuation of the story of the birth of John the Baptizer. Zechariah has not been able to grasp what God is doing in this unexpected birth and has been rendered speechless until all that Gabriel has foretold has taken place. Zechariah is finally able to accept what God has done when he confirms the decision to name the boy John.

Like the father and Zechariah, we would like to believe—despite ourselves. We would like to think that God is working marvels in our own time and place. We desperately want to believe that justice and peace, reconciliation and compassion, are possible. Advent does not demand that we put our doubts aside; Advent offers us a prism in which to see the small, hidden ways in which God acts in our midst and how God often works such marvels through us, despite our doubts and inability to readily see and understand.

The coming of Christ—God becoming one of us out of love for us—calls us to joyful hope in God's constant presence among us, a presence that we are often too jaded or too busy or too overwhelmed to realize. But the notion of "joy to the world" and "peace on earth to all people of good will" that we give at least a hearing to this time of year can be as real and life-giving in every season of the year: in imitating the loving kindness, the compassionate forgiveness, and reconciling humility of Jesus, we make God's living presence a reality in every human heart, in every moment of time, in every gathering place.

Meditation: When have you discovered God at work in your life, despite your initial doubts?

Prayer: Lord Jesus, open our hearts and minds to see what is hidden from us, to hear what the noise and clamor of the world shout down, to embrace the wisdom we cannot yet understand. Through the joys and struggles of family and friendship, may we find our way to your dwelling place by the light of your peace.

December 24: Saturday of the Fourth Week of Advent

"O Holy Night"

Readings: 2 Sam 7:1-5, 8b-12, 14a, 16; Luke 1:67-79

Scripture:
"In the tender compassion of our God
   the dawn from on high shall break upon us,
   to shine on those who dwell in darkness and the
      shadow of death,
   and to guide our feet into the way of peace."
      (Luke 1:78-79)

Reflection: There is a legend in Northern Canada that at midnight on Christmas Eve, a mysterious spirit of peace prevails throughout the world, a spirit so powerful and all-encompassing that even the cattle in the stables and the deer in the forest fall to their knees in adoration. Shakespeare referred to this mysterious Christmas peace in *Hamlet* (act 1, scene 1):

   Some say that whenever that season comes
   Wherein our Savior's birth is celebrated
   The bird of dawn sings all night long;
   They say that no spirit can walk abroad;
   No planet strikes,
   No fairy takes,
   No witch has power to charm,
   So hallowed and gracious is this time.

Zechariah, in his prayer of thanksgiving for the birth of his son John, beautifully sings of this same spirit: "The dawn from on high shall break upon us and shine on those who dwell in darkness."

In a few hours we will begin our Christmas celebration. The squabbles and struggles, the bottom-line pursuits of every day, are put on hold in deference to the good cheer of Christmas. Even nations at war have called a halt to their deadly dealings for this day. For the hours of Christmas, heaven and earth are one.

Meditation: Take a few moments in the busyness of today to see and hear God in the midst of your family and home.

Prayer: Child of Bethlehem, may your coming this Christmas not just "interrupt" our normal flow of time; may we allow Christmas to transform every moment of our lives, as well. May your Spirit prevail in our homes and hearts every night and every day. May the song of the angels be sung and heard with joy in every season of the new year: Peace on earth to all God's people.

SEASON OF CHRISTMAS

December 25: Christmas: the Nativity of the Lord

Christmas Peace

Readings:
   VIGIL: Isa 62:1-5; Acts 13:16-17, 22-25; Matt 1:1-25 (or
      1:18-25)
   MIDNIGHT: Isa 9:1-6; Titus 2:11-14; Luke 2:1-14
   DAWN: Isa 62:11-12; Titus 3:4-7; Luke 2:15-20
   DAY: Isa 52:7-10; Heb 1:1-6; John 1:1-18 (or 1:1-5, 9-14)

Scripture:
And suddenly there was a multitude of the heavenly host
            with the angel,
   praising God and saying:
      "Glory to God in the highest,
         and on earth peace to those on whom his favor
            rests." (Luke 2:11, 13-14)

Reflection: During the first and second centuries, the Roman
Empire enjoyed a period of relative prosperity and tranquil-
ity. In one of the great marketing campaigns of history, Cae-
sar Augustus was hailed as a "god" and the "savior of the
world" for the peace he enforced.

   And enforce it he did. "Peace" meant everyone in their
place, everyone bowing to the power and authority of the
emperor. The celebrated Roman peace was built largely on
intimidation and violence against the vulnerable, the poor,
and the powerless. It was a tense, anxious, costly "peace."

And then, one night in a backwater of the great empire, a new vision of peace appeared. It was peace centered on that perfect love between a mother and her newborn child. It was peace that brought together heaven and earth.

The song heard over the village that night proclaimed the peace that would be the nucleus of the kingdom this child would initiate.

Peace is not just the absence of strife but the presence of compassion and forgiveness. Peace is not fearful passivity but loving perseverance to reconcile and heal. Peace is not enforced by one's power but celebrated in mutual respect and generosity. Peace is not the province of the powerful but the responsibility of all "men and women of good will." Peace exalts humility, poverty, simplicity, service. The economy of peace is built on justice for all and the dignity of the most vulnerable.

Today the peace of God dawns. God's love takes on a human face and heart and body. The work of building God's kingdom of peace begins on this Christmas Day.

Meditation: In what concrete ways can you transform "peace" from an absence of conflict into God's peace of generosity, forgiveness, and humility?

Prayer: Welcome, O Child of Bethlehem! Fill our empty hearts with your Father's peace. May your Spirit make us ministers of that peace, enabling us to become God's "people of good will.

"The Hands and Feet of Jesus"

Readings: Acts 6:8-10; 7:54-59; Matt 10:17-22

Scripture:
As they were stoning Stephen, he called out
  "Lord Jesus, receive my spirit." (Acts 7:59)

Reflection: The murders shocked the world in August of 2010.

The team of ten—six Americans, one German, one Briton, and two Afghans—had travelled the unforgiving mountains and rain-swollen rivers of Afghanistan to do what they loved: helping the chronically ill and caring for children in this desolate region, to be of service to a people they had come to love and respect. They were returning to Kabul after two weeks of working in the mountainous North when gunmen attacked them. The Taliban claimed responsibility for the massacre, saying they were Christian missionaries trying to convert Afghans.

But family and friends said the claim is absurd. The leaders of the group had spent more than thirty years in the region; they knew the risks and were careful. They were unarmed; they went about their work quietly. While they were men and women of deep faith, they were experienced and smart enough to know that they couldn't survive in a place like Afghanistan trying to convert people.

As the father of one of the victims said, "They try to be the hands and feet of Jesus, not the mouth of Jesus."

From the days of Stephen, martyrs throughout the centuries have given their lives for the sake of Gospel compassion and justice. Even in our time, men and women like the ten murdered in Afghanistan in the summer of 2010 pay the price for their witness to the Risen One. They understand, as did Stephen, that baptism makes a claim on us, that if we are real disciples of Jesus we must do the work of Jesus: to love, to heal, to lift up. They realize that the gift of faith requires justice, compassion, and forgiveness. They accept the reality that the Gospel that begins in a Bethlehem stable continues on to the tree of the cross on a hillside outside of Jerusalem. But they carry on in the joy and assurance that their crucifixions and stonings will be vehicles of Easter resurrection.

Meditation: Have you ever paid a price for trying to be the "hands and feet" of Jesus?

Prayer: Father of all that is good, fill us with your Spirit of justice and mercy as you filled your son Stephen. Help us to overcome our own doubts and fears, the ridicule and criticism, the rejection and isolation we encounter in our struggle to be your disciples. May we imitate your example of humble servanthood, as did Stephen, so that we may be "your hands and feet" for all our brothers and sisters in you.

December 27: Saint John, Apostle and Evangelist

Birth and Rebirth

Readings: 1 John 1:1-4; John 20:1a, 2-8

Scripture:
They both ran, but the other disciple ran faster than Peter
   and arrived at the tomb first;
   he bent down and saw the burial cloths there. . . .
   [H]e saw and believed. (John 20:4-5, 8a)

Reflection: Two days ago we stood at the entrance of a Bethlehem stable with a band of shepherds, peering inside to see
a newborn child, wondering what this mysterious birth means.

Today we stand with Peter and Mary and the "other disciple" and look inside an empty tomb, wondering what has
happened.

The story that begins with wonder and hope seems to end
in confusion and terror, but what God begins in the birth of
a child God continues in the rebirth of that child on Easter
morning.

And God continues the story in our own births and rebirths. As the unnamed disciple comes to understand when
he sees the burial wrappings on the ground, our God is a
God of new beginnings, of the constant ability to start again,
of love that knows neither conditions nor limits. The God
who is revealed in Jesus is not about death but about birth—
and rebirth and resurrection.

At Christmas we discover new hope; we "behold" new possibilities for justice, for peace, for forgiveness in our Advent lives. At Easter, we are re-created in such hope; we no longer just "behold" Christ but we embrace and are embraced in his life, death, and resurrection. As we peer into the empty tomb with Mary and Peter and the unnamed disciple, we are as confused and scared as they are. But let their discovery open our imaginations to the possibilities; let the light that illuminates the tomb that can no longer hold Jesus illuminate our hearts to see our lives transformed in God's grace; let the Spirit of God release in us hope that we dare not trust, joy that we fear will be betrayed, dreams that we are resigned to keep hidden and unrealized.

The Child of Bethlehem, the Risen One of Easter morning, is with us in our own time and place, in our own deaths and resurrections, enabling us to realize Advent's hopes and promises in the reality of Easter light.

Meditation: What element of your Christmas prayer or celebration would you most like to continue into the new year? How can you do it?

Prayer: God of beginnings, help us to live in the hope and optimism of Christmas. As we journey with your Son in reading and praying his Gospel in the weeks ahead, may we rediscover your reconciling love in his parables and healings; may we enter, heart and soul, into his "passing over" from life to eternity. May the promise of his birth at Christmas be realized in our own rebirths in the fulfillment of your Easter promise.

The Coventry Carol

Readings: 1 John 1:5–2:2; Matt 2:13-18

Scripture:
When Herod realized that he had been deceived by
    the magi,
  he became furious.
He ordered the massacre of all the boys in Bethlehem and
    its vicinity
  two years old and under
  in accordance with the time he had ascertained from the
    magi. (Matt 2:16)

Reflection: One of the oldest songs of the Christmas season
is "The Coventry Carol," a lullaby sung by the mothers of
the children slain by the tyrant Herod. The anguished mothers (who refer to themselves as "sisters" in the song) mourn
for their innocent babies, killed in the jealous Herod's insane
slaughter to destroy the Christ Child.

  In the earliest version of the text we have, written down
by Robert Croo in 1534, the mothers sing:

    O sisters, too, how may we do
    for to preserve this day
    this poor youngling
    for whom we sing.

bye-bye, lully lullay.
Lully, lullay, thou little tiny child,
bye-bye, lully lullay.

Mothers and fathers of every time and place mourn and continue to mourn for their sons and daughters who are massacred in acts of terrorism and war. They grieve for their children who die of starvation and disease. They cry out for justice for the innocent victims of drunk drivers, urban violence, and racism. Every era of history—including our own—has witnessed the suffering of its own Holy Innocents.

God dies in the death of every innocent child who is destroyed in history's Palestines of self-absorbed Herods. In the dawning of Christ, God calls us to transform the destruction of the Holy Innocents into the eternal season of God's peace and justice.

Meditation: How can you ease the suffering of an "innocent" you know? What injustices can you address that will restore God's justice to your corner of the kingdom?

Prayer: Father of compassion, help us to embrace in our care the innocent victims of war, neglect, and addiction. May their lamentations haunt our hearts and compel our spirits to make our world a safe and nurturing place for all your children.

The Parents of the Bride

Readings: 1 John 2:3-11; Luke 2:22-35

Scripture:
[T]he parents of Jesus took him up to Jerusalem
to present him to the Lord. . . .
[Simeon] took him into his arms and blessed God,
    saying:
". . . my own eyes have seen the salvation
which you have prepared in the sight of every people,
a light to reveal you to the nations
    and the glory of your people Israel."
The child's father and mother were amazed at what was
    said about him. (Luke 2:22, 28, 30-33)

Reflection: They sit together in the front pew, the mother
and father of the bride, holding the other's hand tightly
throughout the wedding service. They share smiles and not
a few tears as their beloved daughter begins a new life with
her husband, a terrific guy they already love as a son.

As the liturgy unfolds, they see much more than just a
beautiful bride in an exquisite gown: They see the beautiful
baby they brought home after a difficult pregnancy and an
anything-but-easy delivery; the six-year-old triumphantly
sounding out the words in her first-grade reader; the thirteen-
year-old on the threshold of womanhood; the moody sixteen-

year-old perpetually exasperated at her hopelessly uncool parents' inability to understand *anything*; the eighteen-year-old off to college and her first taste of freedom—and its costs; the twenty-four-year-old making her way in the world. It was an exciting, fun, terrifying ride, this adventure in parenthood.

Mary and Joseph begin their "ride" as parents by bringing their newborn Son to the temple to present him to the Lord, to incorporate him into the life and traditions of their faith. Terrified and excited like most parents, Mary and Joseph seek to give their Son the best they have—their faith and its values they cherish. We seek to give our own children the best that we have, as well. May we recommit ourselves this Christmas to giving our sons and daughters our faith in the God who loves us so that they may grow "and become strong, filled with wisdom; and the favor of God . . . upon [them]" (Luke 2:40).

Meditation: What has been your most fulfilling moment in raising your own children, or what has been your most rewarding moment teaching or caring for a child?

Prayer: Lord Jesus, the light of God's love, illuminate our hearts and homes this Christmas. As parents, as brothers and sisters, as family members, may we reflect for one another your living presence of compassion, peace, and mercy as we walk together to the dwelling place of your Father.

December 30: Feast of the Holy Family
(Catholic Church)

Sixth Day in the Octave of Christmas
(Episcopal Church)

"Lit"

Readings: Sir 3:2-6, 12-14; Col 3:12-21; Luke 2:22-40

Scripture:
Simeon blessed them and said to Mary his mother,
"Behold, this child is destined
for the fall and rise of many in Israel,
and to be a sign that will be contradicted
—and you yourself a sword will pierce—
so that the thoughts of many hearts may be revealed."
(Luke 2:34-35)

Reflection: *Lit* is Mary Karr's best-selling memoir of her descent into alcoholism and madness and her inspiring resurrection.

Dev is Mary's five-year-old son, the light of Mary's train-wreck of a life. Mary recounts an episode in which her mother comes to visit. Mary's mother has been fighting her own demons of alcoholism and depression. The visit does not go well. Grandma becomes very impatient with Dev over a cookie. She threatens Dev for what she sees as the boy's insolent behavior, before Mary intervenes.

When Mary puts Dev to bed that night, she asks Dev if he was scared that Grandma would hurt him.

Dev gives his mom a puzzled look. Why would he be scared of Grandma hurting him? "Mom," he tells Mary, "you'd never allow that to happen."

While we may not be able to give our children everything we would like, the most important thing we can give them is love—love that is complete and unconditional, love that can be trusted and relied upon, love that endures in good times and bad. As recounted in the gospels, Mary, Joseph, and the Child's struggle as a family was filled with heartache, fear, misunderstanding, and doubt, but together they created a family of love and compassion, of nurture and acceptance, of trust and support that enabled them to cope with the challenges of Simeon's disturbing prophecy. Within our own families the love of God enables us to make our way through life in all its disappointments and complexities. As we gather as families this during this Christmas season, may we take on again the hard work of being family to one another.

Meditation: Has there been a time when love enabled your family to overcome some crisis or adversity?

Prayer: Loving Father, embrace our family in your loving providence. In times of crisis and tension, bless our families with the hope of your consolation and forgiveness; in times of joy and growth, instill in us a spirit of thankfulness, never letting us forget that you are Father of us all.

December 31: Seventh Day in the Octave of Christmas

The Continuing Conversation

Readings: 1 John 2:18-21; John 1:1-18

Scripture:
And the Word became flesh
   and made his dwelling among us. (John 1:14)

Reflection: "The Word became flesh," writes the evangelist John in the beautiful prologue to his gospel. In the original Greek text, the term used for "Word" is *logos*. But *logos* means much more than just a combination of letters that conveys the idea of a thing or action.

Among its many meanings, *logos* is a conversation, a dialogue, an exchange of understandings, a sharing of wisdom, a narrative or story. John's use of the word *logos* portrays Christ as God's ongoing conversation with humankind, an exchange that continues despite the horrors of history, our doubts and misunderstandings, even the crucifixion of the *logos* itself. God's *logos* is not a static, limited word but a dynamic communication in the language of compassion and charity, the letters of sacrament, the rhetoric of ethics and morality. The conversation takes place despite the noise in our lives, the doubts we fear, the anger and disappointments that intimidate us from responding. God is not detached or removed from the human experience; in God's *logos*, the Christ, the Holy One continues to engage us in the dialogue of reconciliation and grace. God speaks in all the "-ologies" of our universe: biology, psychology, sociology.

Christmas is the continuation of the conversation God began with the first spark of creation. God's part of the conversation becomes human in the person of his Christ; God continues to engage us in this dialogue in the Spirit of wisdom and grace.

Meditation: How can you respond to God's *logos* in the year ahead?

Prayer: Open our hearts and enable our spirits to hear your Word and respond to your *logos* in our midst, O God. May we find the words to respond to your Word of compassion; may we learn the language of reconciliation and mercy; may we continue your narrative of peace and justice.

January 1: Solemnity of Mary, Mother of God
(Catholic Church)

The Holy Name
(Episcopal Church)

Christmas Memories

Readings: Num 6:22-27; Gal 4:4-7; Luke 2:16-21

Scripture:
And Mary kept all these things,
   reflecting on them in her heart. (Luke 2:19)

Reflection: Christmas has become the marker for family histories. We remember many of our family's milestones in terms of Christmas: our first Christmas in our new house, our child's first Christmas; the Christmas he was away fighting in Iraq; the Christmas the family spent by her bedside. Many of our Christmas cards include photographs of how the children have grown in the past year and letters bringing family and friends up-to-date on the news of the last twelve months.

On this New Year's Day, we begin to gather up the memories of the Christmas just past with family and friends. We all have a favorite moment from the last few days that will forever mark Christmas 2011; we may also have a moment that gave us pause, to see our lives and our relationships in ways we may not have realized before.

Today's gospel reading contains that wonderful observation from Luke: "Mary kept all these things, reflecting on them in her heart." Scholars have wondered for centuries what led Luke to include that line in his text. Some have suggested that the author of Luke may have met Mary and talked with her about the events of her son's birth.

Our memories are important to us. We learn from them, we are formed by them, we are inspired by them. Remembering can be a powerful form of prayer, enabling us to discern the will of God in our lives as we struggle to make sense of the peaks and valleys we have traveled. Like any loving parent, Mary certainly replayed over and over again the events we read about in the Christmas gospels, constantly trying to discern the will of God as her son's ministry unfolded.

So do not pack away all your Christmas memories. Keep some of the cards and photos nearby. Rejoice in the love of family and friends, lifting them up in prayer. Resolve to heal the hurts and cross the chasms that separate you from others.

Meditation: What is your favorite moment from the last week? What was your biggest disappointment or hurt and how can you make that situation better next Christmas?

Prayer: O God, Giver of all good things, may we embrace a spirit of prayer that begins with realizing your love in the midst of family and friends. Like Mary, may our Christmas memories be the beginning of our prayers of gratitude; may our remembrances of Christmases past teach us your work of compassion and reconciliation.

January 2

John of the Fourth Gospel

Readings: 1 John 2:22-28; John 1:19-28

Scripture:
John answered them,
  "I baptize with water;
  but there is one among you whom you do not recognize,
  the one who is coming after me,
  whose sandal strap I am not worthy to untie."
    (John 1:27)

Reflection: The portrait of John in the Fourth Gospel is much different from the Baptizer we read about in the Synoptics: no eccentric figure clad in camel skins, surviving on locusts and wild honey; no mad rants against the religious establishment; no angry admonitions to those who approached him for baptism. The evangelist John presents a much more approachable Baptizer: a serene, focused, reconciling figure who bridges the age of the prophets and the dawning of the Messiah. The writer of the Fourth Gospel presents John as a voice of hope and joy who dedicates himself to giving testimony to the "light."

John is a model of great humility who goes to great lengths to minimize his role in order to enable the people of the Jordan region to recognize the Christ walking among them. In the Fourth Gospel, the Baptizer is the welcoming entryway for many to behold the Lamb of God in their midst. John opens the hearts and spirits of those who come to his baptism to the first light and hope of the Messiah.

Every Advent, John the Baptizer calls us to embrace the meaning of our own baptisms: compassion, forgiveness, justice, selflessness. John, as depicted in the Fourth Gospel, is a model of the prophet's vision of hope and the disciple's humble compassion. As we begin this new year, let us take up John's Advent work: to straighten the crooked roads of our lives, to transform "deserts" barren of love into places of welcome and reconciliation, to gather up the lost and forgotten, to proclaim the coming of God's Christ in our midst.

Meditation: Consider how you might be a "voice" of God's love in this new year.

Prayer: Gracious God, may we take on the work of your prophet John in this new year: may every kindness and generosity we extend mirror your Christ's presence in our midst; may we joyfully take on the hard work of creating a highway through the rugged lands of estrangement and alienation; may we be effective "voices" proclaiming the good news that you have come.

January 3

The Little Chapel that Could

Readings: 1 John 2:29–3:6; John 1:29-34

Scripture:
John the Baptist saw Jesus coming toward him and said,
  "Behold, the Lamb of God, who takes away the sin of
    the world. . . .
I did not know him,
  but the reason why I came baptizing with water
  was that he might be made known to Israel."
    (John 1:29, 31)

Reflection: Across the street from the site of Ground Zero in New York City stands historic St. Paul's Chapel. St. Paul's was completed in 1766 and is the oldest public building in continuous use in Manhattan.

Ten years ago, the small church miraculously survived the collapse of the towers in the horror of 9/11. The church immediately became a godsend of respite and refreshment for the thousands of police officers, firefighters, and rescue workers at Ground Zero. St. Paul's clergy and congregation coordinated volunteers and donations of food to provide hundreds of rescue workers with everything from coffee and meals to eye drops, clean underwear, and a place to catch a little sleep.

Three days after the attack, the rector of St. Paul's asked engineers if they could somehow get into the St. Paul's bell tower to ring the bell. Despite the devastation around them, two engineers managed to crawl into the wooden tower and, taking an iron rod, beat the bell by hand twelve times. The firemen and volunteers heard the bell, removed their hats and helmets, and paused. In telling the story to the congregation the following Sunday, the rector said: "Now, God willing, we hope to ring [the bell at St. Paul's] at 12 noon every day as long as we exist, remembering to announce to the world, 'God reigns.'"

In opening their doors to the rescue and recovery workers at the site of the World Trade Center devastation, the St. Paul's congregation took up the cry of the Baptizer: *Behold, the Lamb of God. Behold, God is in our midst.* Every one of us has been called to declare to our contemporaries that Christ, the Lamb of God, has come. John declared his witness in preaching and baptizing at the Jordan; our witness can be declared in less vocal but no less effective vehicles: in our unfailing compassion for others, in our uncompromising moral and ethical convictions, in our everyday sense of joy and purpose.

Meditation: Consider how you can take up John's cry that God is in our midst.

Prayer: Christ Jesus, the Lamb of God, may we behold your presence in our midst in every moment of the New Year. May your Spirit transform our perspective and actions so that we may bring to reality your reign of righteousness and reconciliation in our time and place.

January 4: Saint Elizabeth Ann Seton
(Catholic Church)

Mrs. Seton of Philadelphia

Readings: 1 John 3:7-10; John 1:35-42

Scripture:
John was standing with two of his disciples,
  and as he watched Jesus walk by, he said,
  "Behold, the Lamb of God." (John 1:35-36)

Reflection: She was born into the cream of Philadelphia society two years before the signing of the Declaration of Independence. But she came to realize the fragility of life with the death of her mother when she was only three. Her father's second wife wanted nothing to do with her and her sister, so they lived for a time with an uncle. She survived those dark days by her love of literature and poetry, music, the outdoors, and a natural inclination to the spiritual.

She married a young man from an established Philadelphia family. She was a rock of stability and compassion not only for her family and friends but for the poor and sick of the city, especially widows with small children.

Then her world fell apart again. Her husband's business was failing and she worked with him to save it, but to no avail. The stress contributed to her husband's death. At the age of thirty, she was widowed, penniless, with five young children to support. She kept her family together working as a teacher and running a small boarding house.

Inspired by a Catholic family who helped her and her family, she entered the Catholic Church.

When her children were grown, she continued her work as a teacher. The Sulpician Fathers asked her to come to Baltimore and start a school for girls. That school became the first Catholic school for girls in the United States. She and her companions became the Sisters of Charity, the first American women's religious order.

Today we celebrate the feast day of this remarkable woman, the first native-born American citizen to be canonized, St. Elizabeth Ann Bayley Seton.

Elizabeth Ann Seton did extraordinary things in ordinary circumstances. In every dimension and challenge of her life, she responded to Jesus' call to every disciple of every time and place to take on God's work of reconciliation. "God has given us a great deal to do," St. Elizabeth wrote to a friend, "and I have always and hope always to prefer his work to my own."

Meditation: What ordinary things that you do in your typical day can be manifestations of God's love?

Prayer: God of graciousness, in her life as spouse, mother, teacher, and religious, your daughter Elizabeth Ann Seton pointed to the Lamb of God in the midst of her family, her city, her schools, and her community. May the light of your Christ and the grace of your Spirit enable us to reveal your love within our own homes and schools and workplaces.

January 5

The Patience to See

Readings: 1 John 3:11-21; John 1:43-51

Scripture:
Philip found Nathanael and told him,
> "We have found the one about whom Moses wrote in
> the law,
> and also the prophets, Jesus, son of Joseph, from
> Nazareth."

But Nathanael said to him,
> "Can anything good come from Nazareth?"

Philip said to him, "Come and see." (John 1:45-46)

Reflection: A young man sought a position with a master jeweler, but the jeweler brushed him off. The young man pleaded for a chance. The jeweler finally relented: "Be here tomorrow."

The next morning the master jeweler placed a piece of beautiful, expensive jade in the boy's hand and told him to study it. The jeweler then went about his work. All day long the boy sat quietly and waited, holding the jade.

The following morning the jeweler again placed the jade stone in the boy's hand and told him to hold it. On the third, fourth, and fifth days, the jeweler repeated the exercise and the instructions.

On the sixth day the young man finally spoke up: "Sir, when I am going to learn something?"

"You'll learn in time," the master replied.

Several more days went by and the young man's frustration continued to mount. One morning as the jeweler beckoned for the boy to hold out his hand, he was about to blurt out that he could no longer continue. But the instant the stone touched his fingers, the young man exclaimed without looking at his hand, "Wait. This is not the same jade stone."

The master peered over his glasses, smiled, and said, "You have begun to learn."

In today's gospel, the first disciples are invited to look with a new perspective, to see what they had not realized before, to realize who is in their midst. That same invitation is extended to us, the disciples of Jesus in this time. The challenge of discipleship is to discern and respond to that call within our own lives, in the context of our own experiences. Such discernment demands patience and attention that we may not be used to. Jesus dares us to come and see and to follow him. Christ promises us, if we seek it, God's grace enabling us to open our eyes and hearts to behold the life and love of God in our mist.

Meditation: When or where have you found God or the things of God in an unexpected time or place?

Prayer: Remove the fear that darkens our vision, Lord Jesus, that we may recognize the light of your compassion and the wisdom of your justice in even the most unexpected places. With humility of heart and generosity of spirit, may we come to behold your presence in every moment of our lives.

January 6

"The Spirit Descends"

Readings: 1 John 5:5-13; Mark 1:7-11

Scripture:
On coming up out of the water he saw the heavens being
    torn open
    and the Spirit, like a dove, descending upon him.
And a voice came from the heavens,
"You are my beloved son; with you I am well pleased."
    (Mark 1:10-11)

Reflection: Father spends most days in the monastery work-room patiently cutting pieces of cloth that his brother monks will sew to make beautiful vestments and altar cloths. He has served his Benedictine community in every way possible: as the lowliest novice, as a teacher, as a parish priest, and as abbot of the community. Now, in his eighty-ninth year, he continues to serve whenever and wherever he can. To know this monk is to meet someone *upon whom God's spirit has descended.*

To watch this gifted teacher work so patiently and lovingly with her first-graders is to watch a teacher's teacher. To open up these young minds to the wonders of reading and writing and numbers is her joy. Years from now, her students will remember her as a woman of caring, warmth, and compassion *upon whom God's spirit has descended.*

He has had to grow up fast. Because of his father's illness and death and his mother's trying to keep the family together, money is always tight. For a sixteen-year-old, he has an adult sense of responsibility to his mother and younger brother and sister. Whatever money he earns from his after-school job he places on the kitchen table. Mom never asked for or expected it; as far as he's concerned, it's just the right thing to do. Oh, he's a teenager, with all the awkwardness, scorn for everything that is uncool, and devotion to music that is loud, new, and fast. He'd look at you as if you had two heads if you even suggested that *upon him God's spirit has descended.*

In all the accounts of Jesus' baptism, the four evangelists use a similar description of the scene at the Jordan: the Spirit of God "descends" upon him and hovers "like a dove" over his every word and action. God's Spirit resides within Jesus; the peace, compassion, and love of God are a constant presence in this carpenter from Nazareth. That same Spirit "descends" upon us in our baptisms, making us disciples of God's Christ, voices of God's justice, and ministers of God's work of reconciliation.

Meditation: What do you sense the Spirit of God calling you to do in some difficult situation in your life?

Prayer: May your Spirit descend upon us, O God, and lift us out of the waters of our baptisms to begin the work of discipleship. Prompted by your Spirit, let us imitate your Son's humility and servanthood and mirror his Gospel of reconciliation and justice.

January 7

The Changing of Wine

Readings: 1 John 5:14-21; John 2:1-11

Scripture:
There was a wedding at Cana in Galilee. . . .
[T]he headwaiter called the bridegroom and said to him,
"Everyone serves the good wine first,
and when people have drunk freely, an inferior one;
but you have kept the good wine until now." (John 2:1, 10)

Reflection: The marriage begins with champagne on the magical evening of the wedding reception.

But over time, the wine changes.

It becomes a much cheaper vintage as spouses struggle to build a home together. It is replaced by formulas and juice boxes and medicines as they raise their children. With every milestone, with every crisis, the vintage is patience and forgiveness; with every check written to cover the mortgage, insurance, and tuition, selflessness and generosity are the spirits shared in chipped glasses.

The wine tastes sweeter with the grandchildren and the opportunities to help a new family get started.

The wine becomes increasingly bitter and hard with the visits to the doctor, the long wait for the test results, the necessary changes in lifestyle, the round-the-clock care. And eventually they sip their last glass together until they find places next to each other at the wedding banquet of heaven.

92   *Season of Christmas*

In marriages where Christ is the always-welcomed Wedding Guest, the wine of compassion and understanding, of humble love and generous grace, never runs out. The wine served at the marriage feast—a feast that continues over many years from the banquet table to the family dinner table to the workbench to the play table to the quiet table for two—is always "new" and richer and sweeter with every glass poured and shared.

Throughout Scripture, God speaks of his love for humanity in terms of espousal. Christ, who performed his first miracle at a wedding, called himself "the Bridegroom" who comes to bring his people to the wedding feast of the Father. As ministers of the marriage sacrament, husbands and wives, in their love for one another, help all of us to realize the great love of God the Father and Christ his Son, the Bridegroom. In homes where each member of the household works selflessly and humbly to create a place of ready safety and forgiveness for one another, the sign of God's love for all humanity is made manifest.

Meditation: Recall the most recent time you experienced the compassion of God in the midst of your family.

Prayer: O God, Father of all, help us to make our own homes "feasts" of your compassion and forgiveness. May every act of kindness and consolation we offer be the wine of the feast; may we transform every table and space into banquet tables where your love among us is celebrated.

January 8: The Epiphany of the Lord

"Into the Woods"

Readings: Isa 60:1-6; Eph 3:2-3a, 5-6; Matt 2:1-12

Scripture:
When Jesus was born in Bethlehem of Judea . . .
  behold, magi from the east arrived in Jerusalem, saying,
  "Where is the newborn king of the Jews?
We saw his star at its rising
  and have come to do him homage." (Matt 2:1-2)

Reflection: In the Broadway musical *Into the Woods*, composer Stephen Sondheim and playwright James Lapine recast the familiar stories of Jack in the Beanstalk, Cinderella, Little Red Riding Hood, Rapunzel, and an original tale about a baker and his wife who are childless. In the beginning of the story, all the characters express their wishes for happiness: a handsome prince to marry, a warm home and enough to eat, a child to love. But in order to realize those dreams, the characters have to travel "into the woods" to confront the wolves, witches, giants, and charlatans that thwart their dreams.

  In their individual journeys through the woods, the characters discover that life is not a fairy tale. They come to see that the line between dreams and nightmares is a fine one. They realize that the real monsters they must defeat are selfishness and greed, that the most potent spells they have to break are fear and self-deception.

94   *Season of Christmas*

The Epiphany gospel recounts a similar journey: Like the fairy-tale characters seeking "happily ever after" in their trek into the woods, the magi set out to find the Messiah-King the world longed for. It is a journey filled with challenges, questions, and obstacles that ends, finally, in an experience of *epiphany*—the realization of God in their midst.

Every human life is a journey. As we make our way through the time God has given us, we seek signs of God in our midst; we seek happiness that is authentic and real. In the end, we come to realize that it is love in all its joy and sorrow, in all its demands and gifts, that makes us real and whole human beings. In encountering the Christ, the magi behold the love of God in their midst.

May our encounter with Christ be a constant epiphany of re-creating and transforming our lives in the love of Emmanuel, "God with us."

Meditation: In your own life's journey, what has been the most difficult lesson you have learned? In what ways was God revealed to you in that "epiphany"?

Prayer: Christ Jesus, the very manifestation of God's love, be with us on our journey to your Father's dwelling place. Open our eyes to realize the "epiphanies" of your love along our way; illuminate the path we journey by the star of your compassion. Send your Spirit to guide us over the steep terrain, across the hopeless deserts, and through the terrifying nights to make our way to the light of your kingdom.

Water, Bread, and a Flower

Readings: Isa 42:1-4, 6-7; Acts 10:34-38; Mark 1:7-11

Scripture:
This is what [John] proclaimed:
"One mightier than I is coming after me. . . .
I have baptized you with water;
he will baptize you with the Holy Spirit." (Mark 1:7a, 8)

Reflection: A cup of water has very little worth. Two parts hydrogen, one part oxygen. It is so ordinary, so common. But it can unlock the life-giving harvest of a planted seed; it can bring healing to the sick and dying; it can revive the tired, the faded, the exhausted.

A piece of bread is the most basic of foods; it is hardly a feast. But when shared lovingly and gratefully with the hungry, the poor, the forgotten, a single piece of bread is the banquet of heaven.

A single flower. But one rose given to one's beloved, even a dandelion given by a child to his mother, says, "I love you," more eloquently than the most beautiful sonnet.

A cup of water, a piece of bread, a flower. Of themselves, not much of anything. So simple, so ordinary. Yet each one can manifest, in its own way, in its own good time, compassion, forgiveness, and love that are no less than that of God.

The mystery of the incarnation—the meaning of Christmas, the wonder of the Epiphany events of Jesus' birth, baptism, and first miracle—is that nothing is so ordinary that it cannot be sacred, nothing is so common that it cannot be holy when that thing becomes a means for expressing the love of God. In becoming human in Jesus, God makes holy our very humanness; in taking on our human nature, God sanctifies our very lives. When we become vehicles of God's love, when we become the means for manifesting God's presence in our world, we become sacred and holy, as well.

May all that we hold, may all that we touch, may all that we are, realize the true miracle of the incarnation—that we and our world are holy and sacred in the sight of God, our Father and Creator.

Meditation: In what specific ways is your everyday, ordinary life made holy by God's grace?

Prayer: O God, the world is filled with the radiance of your glory. May we experience your holiness in every moment and activity of the new year; may we be transformed by your love experienced in the compassion and forgiveness we give and receive from family and friends; may we be lifted up in hope and raised to new joy in the realization of your compassion in our midst.

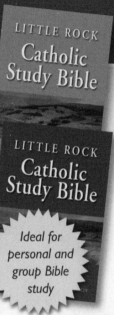